AF231846

The First 60 Seconds In Car Sales

A Proven Meet and Greet System to Build Trust and Start More Conversations

Bruce Huddleston

Bedrock Heritage Publishing

Published by:

Bedrock Heritage Publishing

A Division of Life Guidance Consulting LLC

Tyler, Texas

www.bedrockheritagepublishing.com

info@bedrockheritagepublishing.com

ISBN: 978-1-972179-10-9

ISBN: 978-1-972179-58-1 (EPUB)

Part of the Car Sales Survival Series

Printed in the United States of America

DISCLAIMER

This book is based on the author's personal and professional experiences, observations, and opinions accumulated over a 35-year career in the automotive industry. It is intended for educational and informational purposes only.

The stories and anecdotes contained in this book are drawn from real-world situations encountered throughout the author's career. However, names, identifying details, specific circumstances, employer names, dealership names, and individual characteristics have been changed, omitted, combined, or fictionalized to protect the privacy of the individuals involved. Any resemblance to specific living persons, current or former employers, or existing businesses is coincidental and unintentional.

No individual, dealership, organization, or employer referenced or implied in the stories within this book has reviewed, approved, or endorsed the content herein. The recollections and characterizations presented are solely the author's own perspective and memory of events and do not constitute a factual record, legal testimony, or statement of fact regarding any identifiable person or entity.

The sales strategies, techniques, and professional advice presented in this book reflect the author's personal approach and experience. Individual results will vary based on experience, effort, market conditions, dealership policies, and other factors beyond the author's control. Nothing in this book constitutes a guarantee of income, employment, or professional outcome.

The author and publisher have made reasonable efforts to ensure the accuracy of information presented at the time of writing. The author and publisher make no representations or warranties regarding the completeness, accuracy, or current applicability of the information contained herein, and expressly disclaim any liability arising from the use or application of the content of this book.

By reading this book, you acknowledge and agree that the author and publisher shall not be liable for any damages, losses, or claims arising directly or indirectly from the use of or reliance upon any information contained herein.

*To the sales professionals who understand that success
does not begin with the pitch.
It begins with the moment before it.*

Free Bonus for Readers

Your Complete Digital Script Library

As a reader of The First 60 Seconds in Car Sales, you have access to the complete digital version of every script and checklist in this book — formatted, printable, and ready to customize in your own voice.

Visit the link below, enter your email address, and receive:

The Complete First 60 Seconds Script Library

All scripts from this book are in a digital, editable format

The Full First Minute Checklist

Printable and ready for daily use on the lot

Additional Objection Handling Scenarios

Expanded responses for the toughest opening moments

Access to the full Car Sales Survival Guide Series

Browse and order all titles from the series.

www.carsalessurvivalseries.com/scripts

Enter your email to claim your free reader bonus.

Contents

Introduction   XI

1. The Sale Begins Before the Customer Leaves Their Car   1

2. What Customers Are Already Thinking When They Pull In   4

3. The Ten-Second Rule on the Lot   7

4. How to Approach Without Feeling Pushy   10

5. The Perfect First Sixty Seconds   13

6. Body Language That Builds Instant Trust   16

7. The First Question That Opens Everything   19

8. Common Mistakes That Kill the First Minute   22

9. When Customers Say I'm Just Looking   26

10. The First Sixty Seconds and Customer Confidence   29

11. A Simple Meet and Greet Script for Car Sales   33

12. The Psychology Behind the First Minute   37

13. The First Minute Checklist   41

Conclustion   44

Tips For The Manager   47

Appendix-The Rules   50

Also Available   52

Work With Bruce   54

About the Author   56

A Quick Favor   57

Introduction

Why the First Minute Determines Everything

Most car salespeople think the sale starts when they open their mouth. It doesn't.

It starts the second the customer pulls onto the lot, before you've taken a step. Before you've said a word. The customer is already watching — reading the lot, reading the people standing around, deciding whether this place feels like somewhere they want to be.

By the time they step out of that car, they've already started forming an opinion. Not about the inventory. About you. About whether the person walking toward them is someone they can work with or someone they need to defend themselves against.

I spent thirty-five years in this business. Every level — floor salesperson, finance manager, sales manager, general manager. I've trained hundreds of salespeople and watched thousands of customer interactions. And one thing I've seen over and over is this: the salespeople who struggle almost always struggle in the same place. Not because they don't know the product. Not because they can't close. Because they never figured out how to make a customer comfortable before the conversation started.

That's what this book is about.

Not the pitch. Not the close. The sixty seconds before any of that gets a chance to happen. The moment that determines whether the customer opens up or shuts down. Whether the next hour feels like a productive conversation or an uphill battle against someone who's already decided they don't trust you.

What you'll find in these pages is what I've seen work on the floor and in the training room over thirty-five years of real interactions with real customers. The approach that lowers tension instead of creating it. The body language that communicates confidence without pressure. The first question opens a conversation instead of ending it. The mistakes that kill the first minute — and they're almost always the same mistakes, made by different people, for the same reasons.

Car sales is a relationship business. The vehicle matters. The price matters. Product knowledge matters. But none of that matters if the customer never gets comfortable enough to have a real conversation with you. And that comfort — or the lack of it — gets decided in the first sixty seconds.

Master that minute and have an edge that most salespeople on your floor will never develop.

"The Rule: The sale doesn't begin when you start talking. It begins the moment the customer sees you. Everything after that is either easier or harder, depending on what happened in those first sixty seconds."

The Sale Begins Before the Customer Leaves Their Car

MOST NEW SALESPEOPLE THINK the meet-and-greet starts when they walk up. It doesn't. It starts when the customer pulls in and looks toward the showroom.

From inside their car — before they've turned off the engine, before they've opened the door — they're already watching and scanning the lot and looking at the inventory, the building, and the people standing around. They notice who looks alert. They notice whether a salesperson is leaning against something or scrolling through their phone. They notice whether employees are huddled together talking, completely oblivious to the fact that a customer just pulled in.

All of that shapes how comfortable the customer feels before a single word has been spoken. And it shapes it fast.

The Lot Is Already Talking

Here's something I learned early and never forgot: the environment communicates before the people do. A clean, organized lot with alert professionals says this place takes itself seriously. A lot where the staff looks bored, distracted, or indifferent to arriving customers says the opposite — and it says it before you've had any chance to change the story with words.

Customers arrive already evaluating. They're deciding, based on everything they can see, whether this will be the experience they hoped for or the one they were warned about. The salesperson who understands this doesn't wait for the customer to step out before deciding to be switched on. They're already on. Posture right. Attention on the lot. They look like someone worth walking toward.

Timing the Approach

One of the most important things to understand about those first moments is timing. Customers need a beat after parking to gather themselves. They might be finishing a thought, checking something on their phone, or taking in the environment. That's completely natural.

Approaching before they've even closed the car door is one of the most common mistakes on the lot. It feels aggressive to the customer, no matter your intention. You're thinking: I'm being attentive, I'm showing service. The customer is thinking: I haven't even had a chance to breathe, and someone is already on top of me.

That feeling — being descended upon before you're ready — creates immediate resistance. The guard goes up before the conversation has started, and now you're working against the very thing you were trying to create.

Give them a moment. Let them step out. Let them take a few steps and start to orient themselves. That pause communicates something important without you saying a word: you're not desperate, you're not chasing, and you respect that the customer gets to arrive on their own terms. That patience often makes customers more willing to engage. Not less.

The Acknowledgment From a Distance

While they're settling in, there's one thing you do immediately: acknowledge them. Not by rushing over. By letting them know they've been seen.

A nod. A small wave. A brief "Hi folks, I'll be right with you" from a comfortable distance. That small gesture does something powerful. It tells the customer that help is available while giving them room to breathe. They don't feel ignored or ambushed. They feel noticed — which is exactly what they came in hoping to feel.

Most customers arrive braced for one of two things: being ignored or being jumped on. When you acknowledge them calmly from a distance before you approach, you've already defied both expectations. You've exceeded the bar before the conversation has even started.

"The Rule: The sale begins the moment the customer pulls onto the lot. Be ready before they arrive, because by the time they step out of that car, they've already started deciding how this is going to go."

CHAPTER 2

What Customers Are Already Thinking When They Pull In

To handle the first sixty seconds well, you need to understand something most salespeople never stop to think about: what is the customer feeling before you've done anything?

The honest answer for most customers is a combination of excitement, uncertainty, and caution. They're excited because they're about to look at something they want. They're uncertain because buying a car is a big financial decision with many moving parts they don't fully understand. And they're cautious because someone in their life — a friend, a family member, an experience — has told them to watch out for the pressure.

That caution is the thing you most need to understand. It means the customer arrives with their guard already partially up. Not fully — they came in, after all. But partially. And they're watching for signals that tell them whether their caution was warranted or whether they can relax.

The Questions They're Not Asking Out Loud

From the moment they arrive, customers are running through a quiet checklist. They're not saying these things out loud, but the questions are there.

Is this person going to pressure me? Am I going to get a chance to look around? Can I trust this salesperson? Is this going to be the experience I was warned about?

None of those questions gets answered by your product knowledge or your closing technique. They get answered by how the first sixty seconds feel. By your posture. Your pace. Your tone. Whether you acknowledge the whole group or just the person who spoke first. Whether your opening question feels like an invitation or an interrogation.

Every signal you send in those first sixty seconds is answering those questions. The only question is whether your answers open or close the conversation.

The Trust Gap

Here's the reality of the business you're in: customers know you're trying to sell them something. That's not a secret. They walked onto a car lot, not into a library. The transaction is understood.

What they're trying to figure out is whether you're someone they can trust through the process. Whether you're going to be straight with them. Whether you're going to help them find the right vehicle or just the most profitable one for you.

That determination starts forming in the first minute. Not from what you tell them about the vehicle, but from how you make them feel before you've said anything about the vehicle at all.

A calm voice. Unhurried communication. Respect for personal space. Acknowledging everyone in the group. A question that invites rather than pressures. These are the signals that answer the trust question in your favor. When they show up together in the first sixty seconds, the conversation opens. When they're missing, you're spending the rest of the interaction trying to rebuild trust that should have been established at the beginning.

Every Customer Is Different. Every Customer Has the Same Need.

Not every customer walks in from the same place. Some are excited and ready to engage immediately. Some are methodical—they want information before they talk to anyone. Some are replacing a car they loved, and they're grieving a little. Some are under financial pressure, and they're already stressed before they step out of the car. Some have been burned before, and they're giving the industry a cautious second chance.

What all of them have in common is the same fundamental need: they want to feel like the person in front of them is there to help them, not to extract something from them.

Meeting that need doesn't require knowing their backstory before you approach. It just requires approaching in a way that communicates — through everything you do in that first minute — that you're on their side.

"The Rule: Every customer arrives with a question they haven't asked yet. Your job in the first sixty seconds is to answer it before they do: yes, this is someone I can trust."

CHAPTER 3

THE TEN-SECOND RULE ON THE LOT

First impressions in car sales don't take long. By the time a customer has been watching you for ten seconds, they've already started deciding how they feel about the interaction. Not consciously, not deliberately — automatically, the way people process new situations. They're reading signals and drawing conclusions before either of you has said a word.

Ten seconds sounds like almost nothing. But in that window, a customer can tell whether you look confident or anxious, professional or indifferent, ready to help or just going through the motions. And once those early impressions form, they stick. They shape how the customer receives everything that comes after.

What Gets Read in Ten Seconds

Customers aren't processing complex information in those first ten seconds. They're processing visible signals — the kind that communicate before language gets involved.

Posture is one of the first things they register. A salesperson standing upright, head up, aware of their surroundings, looks like someone who belongs here and knows what they're doing. A salesperson slouched against a vehicle or staring at a phone looks like someone enduring their shift rather than working it.

Movement is another. The pace and manner in which you begin moving toward a customer tells them something immediately. Calm, purposeful movement says confidence. Frantic or overly eager movement says desperation. Customers feel the difference even when they couldn't explain why.

And your face. Your expression is communicating before your mouth is. A relaxed, open expression lowers tension. A flat or distracted expression creates it. You don't need to perform enthusiasm. You need to look like someone who is genuinely glad a customer arrived — because if you're doing this job right, you should be.

The Clock Starts Before You're Ready

Here's the part that trips most salespeople up: you don't get to decide when the clock starts. The customer decides. The moment they see you — from their car window, through the showroom glass, as they walk onto the lot — the evaluation has begun. Not when you notice them. Not when you decide to engage. When they see you.

That means everything you project before you consciously decide to approach is already part of the first impression. Your posture at your desk between customers. The expression on your face when you're not talking to anyone. Whether your phone is in your hand when a car pulls in, it's all part of what the customer is reading.

The professionals who consistently make strong first impressions understand this. They don't wait for a customer to arrive before deciding to be present. They stay present between customers — attentive, composed, ready — because they know the clock can start at any moment.

You Cannot Recover the First Ten Seconds

Some salespeople assume a strong recovery can overcome a weak opening. Sometimes it can. But recovery is harder than getting it right. It takes more time, more effort, more deliberate trust-building to overcome a deficit that never needed to exist.

And some customers don't wait around for the recovery. They make their assessment in ten seconds, decide the experience isn't worth their time, and disengage — either physically by leaving, or emotionally by shutting down while still standing on your lot. The salesperson who spent forty minutes with someone who "wasn't interested" may have been dealing with a customer who, in the first ten seconds, decided they weren't interested and was just being polite while looking for a way out.

The ten-second rule is not a reason to be anxious. It's a reason to be prepared. Know what you're projecting. Make deliberate choices about it. Be ready before the customer arrives. Those three things, done consistently, take care of the first ten seconds without you having to think about them.

"The Rule: Ten seconds. That's how fast the first impression forms on the lot. Be the salesperson they decide they want to talk to before you've opened your mouth."

CHAPTER 4

How to Approach Without Feeling Pushy

ONE OF THE MOST common problems for new salespeople — and plenty of experienced ones too — is figuring out how to approach a customer without making them feel like they're being hunted. Most customers expect some level of sales attention when they walk onto a lot. What they don't want is to feel cornered before they've had a chance to breathe.

The good news is that the line between attentive and aggressive is not as fine as people think. It comes down to three things: timing, pace, and what you communicate when you get there.

Timing the Move

When a customer pulls in and parks, they need a moment. Not five minutes — a moment. Enough time to step out of the car, close the door, and take a look around. During that time, your job is to acknowledge them from a distance — a nod, a small wave, a brief verbal acknowledgment if they're close enough — and then let them settle before you move.

That pause is not passivity. It's professional patience, and customers read it as confidence. A salesperson who gives them that moment is communicating: "I'm not desperate for your business; I'm here to help you when you're ready." That's exactly the impression you want to create before you've said a word of substance.

The salesperson who starts moving the moment the car door opens is communicating something very different: I've been watching for you, and I'm not letting you get away. Even when the intention is genuinely just to be helpful, that's what the speed of the approach says. Customers respond to what they feel, not what you intended.

The Pace of the Walk

Once you're moving, the pace does as much communicating as anything you'll say. Walk at a normal, purposeful pace. Not strolling — that suggests indifference. Not rushing — that suggests desperation. The pace of someone glad a customer arrived and is moving to help them.

Keep your hands visible and relaxed. Head up, eyes forward. Natural eye contact from a reasonable distance, even before you've reached them, communicates that you see them and you're coming to help — not to chase them down.

Stop at a conversational distance. Close enough to talk normally, far enough that they don't feel physically crowded. In most situations, that's roughly an arm's length to six feet. Read the customer as you get close. Some people open up as you approach — they turn toward you, make eye contact, signal they're ready. Others hold their body language slightly closed. Give those people more space.

One Salesperson. Not Two.

This comes up more than you'd expect. Two salespeople see a car pull in at the same time, and both start moving. By the time the customer steps out, they're being approached from two directions simultaneously.

To the customer who doesn't feel like great service. It feels like being cornered. One salesperson approaches. One. If your colleague got up at the same moment, one of you turns around. Sort it out quietly and immediately so the customer only sees one person walking toward them at a normal pace. One person handles the relationship from that moment forward.

FROM THE FLOOR

I was sitting in the front lobby of a dealership I managed — with a glass-front wall and a full view of the lot. A car pulled in. Two salespeople inside saw it at the same time. They both jumped up, ran for the door, and literally shoved each other, trying to get through it first, pushing and shoving like it was a race.

The customers, still in their car, watched every second of this.

The one who won was out of breath when he got there. He stuck his hand out and started talking before he'd even caught his breath, never looked at the wife, never acknowledged the kids in the back seat. Just started in.

The family looked around for a few minutes and left.

When I asked what happened, the salesperson said: "They were just looking."

No. They were watching. And what they watched told them everything they needed to know about what the next hour would feel like. The sprint didn't just cost a deal; it cost a deal. It answered every one of the customer's silent questions about this place — and none of the answers were good.

Confidence Is Not Aggression

Some salespeople hear "don't be pushy" and translate it as "be passive." That's not what this is.

A calm, confident approach is not a weak approach. Customers are far more likely to engage with someone who appears relaxed and in control than someone who appears anxious or aggressive. The goal is to project the quiet confidence of a professional who knows what they're doing and genuinely wants to help—not the frantic energy of someone who needs this deal.

When you approach that way — with purpose, patience, and calm — most customers will meet you there. The guard comes down. The conversation opens. And the first sixty seconds do exactly what they're supposed to do.

"The Rule: Attentive and aggressive are not the same thing. Give the customer a moment, walk with purpose, and arrive as someone they're glad showed up."

CHAPTER 5

THE PERFECT FIRST SIXTY SECONDS

A GREAT FIRST SIXTY seconds is not a performance. It's not a polished routine you run through the same way every time, regardless of who just pulled in. It's a professional sequence — a reliable structure that makes sure the right things happen in the right order — delivered in a way that feels natural because it has become natural through practice.

The goal of the first sixty seconds is not to sell a car. It's to make the customer comfortable enough to have a real conversation. Everything else — the vehicle selection, the numbers, the close — depends on that conversation happening. And that conversation only happens when the customer feels safe enough to start it.

The Sequence

The first sixty seconds follow a clear sequence. Every element has a purpose. None of them is optional.

It starts before you move. Before you take a step toward the customer, you acknowledge them. A nod, a small wave, a brief verbal signal from wherever you are. This tells them they've been seen, help is available, and nobody is going to ambush them. That small gesture does more to lower the customer's guard than anything you'll say in the next sixty seconds.

Then you move. At a normal, purposeful pace. Not rushed, not dragging. Head up, hands relaxed and visible, eyes forward. You're moving toward them the way a professional moves toward someone they're glad to see.

When you arrive at a conversational distance, you introduce yourself. Your name and the dealership name. Said clearly — not mumbled, not rushed. Then comes the most important line in the opening: a service-oriented question that invites the customer to speak rather than pressuring them to commit. "How can I help you today?" It works because it's open, non-threatening, and positions you as someone who is there for them.

Then you stop talking and listen to what they say.

Acknowledge Everyone

If the customer arrived with other people — a spouse, a partner, a parent, a friend — each is acknowledged. Not as an afterthought. In the greeting itself. "Welcome in — good to see you both." Or turn to the person who hasn't been introduced and say: "And you are?"

This matters more than most salespeople realize. The person who didn't speak first is often the person who decides. The wife who's been standing quietly while her husband drives the conversation has veto power that will end the deal in a heartbeat if she doesn't feel respected. I've watched it happen a hundred times. Acknowledging everyone in the group in the first sixty seconds is one of the simplest and highest-value habits in this business.

Ask If They've Been In Before

Early in the greeting — before you go any further — ask this: "Have you been in before, or is this your first time visiting us?"

Non-negotiable. If the customer talked to another salesperson last week or came in three days ago, and you take the up without asking, you're about to invest thirty minutes in a conversation that ends with someone else getting the credit. Ask early, ask cleanly, and handle whatever the answer is professionally. If they have a relationship with someone else at the store, find that person and make the introduction. That's the right move for the customer and for your team.

What It Feels Like When It's Done Right

From the customer's side, a perfect first sixty seconds feels easy. They feel noticed without feeling ambushed. They feel welcomed without feeling pressured. They feel like they're talking to someone calm, competent, and genuinely interested in helping them — not someone who needs their business so badly it's coming off them in waves.

That feeling — easy, comfortable, no pressure — is the foundation for everything else. Get the first sixty seconds right, and the conversation opens naturally. The customer talks more, shares more, and stays more engaged. Get it wrong, and you spend the rest of the interaction trying to claw back ground that was lost before you said hello.

Simple sequence. Consistent execution. Every customer, every time.

"The Rule: The perfect opening is not a performance. It is a sequence done consistently — acknowledge, approach, introduce, ask, and listen. Do it right every time, and the conversation takes care of itself."

CHAPTER 6

BODY LANGUAGE THAT BUILDS INSTANT TRUST

IN CAR SALES, BODY language does more work in the first minute than anything you say. Customers are processing your posture, your movement, your expression, and your eye contact before they've fully registered your words. And what they process in those first nonverbal moments shapes how they receive everything that comes after.

This is not a soft concept. It's a practical one. Every element of your nonverbal presentation either builds the customer's comfort or erodes it. There is no neutral ground. You are always communicating. The only question is whether you're doing it on purpose.

Posture

Posture is the first signal a customer reads from a distance, before you've taken a step toward them. Standing upright with relaxed shoulders says: I'm present, I'm in control of this environment, and I'm capable of helping you.

Slouching against a vehicle, leaning on the showroom wall, standing in a way that looks like you're waiting for your shift to end — that communicates the opposite. Customers don't give you the benefit of the doubt when it comes to posture. They see what they see, and they conclude it instantly.

Check your posture before the lot opens and periodically throughout the day. It drifts when you're tired or distracted. The customer who pulls in at

4:30 in the afternoon deserves the same professional presentation as the one who came in at 10 in the morning.

Eye Contact

Natural eye contact communicates attention and honesty. It tells the customer you are fully present and nothing else is competing for your focus. That matters enormously to someone who walked in half-expecting to feel like an inconvenience.

What you're going for is calm, attentive awareness. Not a stare—not constant eye contact that makes the customer feel examined. But the natural eye contact of someone who is genuinely paying attention. When you're glancing at your phone, looking past them at the lot, or scanning the showroom while they're talking to you, the message is clear: something else is more important than you are right now. Customers feel that immediately.

When you're talking to a group, your eye contact moves. You include everyone. A glance at the spouse, a look toward the friend who came along, a moment of connection with the adult child who's been standing quietly. Each one of those small moments communicates the same thing: I see you, and you matter in this conversation.

Facial Expression

Your face sets the emotional tone of the interaction before a word is spoken. A relaxed, open expression — even a small genuine smile — tells the customer their arrival was a good thing. It communicates welcome before the greeting does.

The flat expression of someone running on autopilot, the distracted look of someone whose mind is somewhere else, the tight expression of someone still carrying the frustration from the last bad interaction — all of these create distance before you've had a chance to do anything right. Customers don't know why the person in front of them looks slightly off. They just know how it makes them feel.

Reset between customers. It takes thirty seconds. Clear the last interaction, adjust your expression, and decide to show up for the next person the way they deserve.

Movement and Hands

How you move communicates as much as how you stand. Quick, jerky movement creates a sense of anxiety or urgency that puts people on edge. Calm, deliberate movement communicates the opposite: everything is under control here, there's no reason to be tense.

What you do with your hands matters too. Fidgeting with keys, holding your phone, shuffling papers as you approach — these communicate distraction. When you're about to greet a customer, your hands should be empty and relaxed. That small thing says something significant: right now, you are the only thing that matters.

Alignment

The most useful way to think about all of this is alignment. Your body should reinforce the message your words are trying to convey. If you're saying "How can I help you?" while standing straight, making natural eye contact, and moving with calm purpose — those things align. The greeting feels authentic.

When words and body language contradict each other, customers feel the disconnect even if they can't name it. Something feels off. That slight discomfort compounds over the course of the interaction and costs you trust you could have had for free.

Pay attention to what your body is saying. Most salespeople don't. The ones who do have an advantage in the first sixty seconds that their competitors never even realize they're missing.

"The Rule: Your body language answers the customer's questions before you open your mouth. Make sure the answers it's giving are the ones that open the conversation."

CHAPTER 7

THE FIRST QUESTION THAT OPENS EVERYTHING

ONCE YOU'VE ACKNOWLEDGED THE customer, approached them at the right pace, introduced yourself, and greeted everyone in the group, you ask a question. And that question, more than almost anything else in the first sixty seconds, determines whether the conversation opens or shuts down.

Most salespeople understand this in theory. In practice, they ask the wrong question anyway. Not because they're trying to create pressure, but because the questions that feel natural in a sales environment are often the ones that feel like pressure to the customer.

The Questions That Close the Conversation

"What are you looking to buy today?"

"Which vehicle are you here to see?"

"What brings you in today?"

None of these is a terrible line. But all of them have the same problem: they ask the customer to declare an intention or commit to a direction before they're ready. The customer just stepped out of their car. They haven't looked at anything yet. They may not know exactly what they want. And even if they do, they're not necessarily ready to tell a stranger within the first thirty seconds of meeting them.

When a customer feels pushed to answer before they're ready, they default to the most protective response available: "I'm just looking." And now you're starting from behind. The wall went up because your question built it.

The Question That Opens the Conversation

"How can I help you today?"

That's it. Four words that change the entire dynamic of the opening.

First, the question is open. It doesn't assume anything about what the customer is there for or what stage of the buying process they're in. It leaves the door wide open for them to answer in whatever terms feel natural to them.

Second, it's service-oriented rather than sales-oriented. "How can I help you?" positions you as someone who is there for the customer. "What are you looking to buy?" positions you as someone focused on the transaction. Customers feel that distinction immediately.

Third, the answer tells you everything you need to know to begin. A customer who says, "I've been looking at the F-250 you have listed online" is ready to engage. A customer who says "We're just starting to look at our options" needs a different approach. A customer who says, "I need to replace my car — mine got totaled this week," has urgency and emotional context that shapes the entire conversation. All of that comes from one open question, voluntarily, because you asked in a way that didn't feel like a trap.

After You Ask, Stop Talking

This is the part that trips up even experienced salespeople. You ask the question — and then you keep talking. You fill the silence. You add a detail. You ask a follow-up before they've answered the first question. You do it because the silence feels uncomfortable, and talking feels like doing something.

Stop. Ask the question and be quiet.

Let the customer answer in their own words at their own pace. Don't interrupt. Don't complete their sentences. Don't nod so aggressively that it looks like you're rushing them toward a conclusion. Just listen. Actually listen — not listening while you're preparing your next line, but listening with the genuine intention of understanding what this person is telling you.

When customers feel heard in the first sixty seconds, something shifts. The guard comes down a little more. The conversation becomes more real. They start talking to you instead of carefully managing what they say to you. That shift — from guarded to open — is worth more than any technique in this book. And it starts with asking one good question and then being quiet enough to hear the answer.

Respond to What They Actually Said

This sounds obvious. It isn't, in practice.

A lot of salespeople ask the opening question, hear the customer's initial answer, and immediately steer toward what they planned to talk about anyway. The customer says they're looking for something reliable for a long commute, and the salesperson is already mentally walking them toward the truck they want to move this week.

The first question only works if you actually use the answer. Listen to what the customer tells you about their situation, needs, timeline, and concerns. Then respond to that. Let their answer shape the next sixty minutes the same way the first sixty seconds shaped their comfort level. They told you exactly how to help them. All you have to do is listen.

"The Rule: The first question either opens the conversation or closes it. Ask how you can help, stop talking, and let the customer tell you everything you need to know."

CHAPTER 8

COMMON MISTAKES THAT KILL THE FIRST MINUTE

MOST LOST CUSTOMERS AREN'T lost at the close or during the negotiation. They're lost in the first minute. Not because the salesperson said something egregiously wrong, but because small habits — habits that feel harmless or even well-intentioned — communicate the wrong thing at the worst possible time.

I've watched these mistakes happen on lots, in showrooms, and in training rooms for thirty-five years. They're consistent. They're common. And they're almost always invisible to the person making them.

Approaching Too Fast

The sprint is the most common mistake on the lot and the one that does the most immediate damage. A car pulls in; the salesperson sees it and moves—fast. They get there before the customer has had time to step out, close the door, or take a breath. The intention is good: they're being attentive, they're showing up. The effect is the opposite.

A customer who gets descended upon before they're ready goes into protection mode immediately. The guard goes up before the conversation starts. Everything that follows is harder because of those first five seconds. Slow down. Let them settle. Acknowledge from a distance. Then approach at a pace that communicates confidence, not desperation.

The Phone Problem

Walking up to a customer while holding your phone is one of the most damaging things you can do in the opening, and it has gotten worse every year. It doesn't matter if you were just checking inventory. It doesn't matter if you put it in your pocket as you stand up. The customer who saw you looking at it ten seconds before you approached has already received the message: something on that screen was more important than they were.

The phone goes away before you approach. Not as you approach. Before. That's not a guideline — it's the standard. A customer who has your undivided attention from the moment you start moving toward them feels it. It costs you nothing, and it communicates something significant.

Ignoring the Group

A couple walks in. The husband speaks first. The salesperson talks to the husband for the next twenty minutes while the wife stands slightly to the side, unacknowledged, feeling invisible. Then she looks at her husband and says she's ready to go.

And the salesperson says, "They were just looking."

No. She was deciding. And the decision she made was that this person wasn't worth doing business with, because he never once looked at her.

Greet every person in the group. Every time. Without exception. The one you ignore is almost always the one who decides.

Carrying the Last Interaction Forward

Customer-facing work is emotionally demanding. Not every interaction goes well. Some customers are rude. Some deals fall apart at the worst possible moment. Some mornings start with a conversation that puts you somewhere you don't want to be.

And then a new customer pulls in. If you walk straight from the last interaction to this one without resetting, this customer absorbs everything you're carrying with you. Your tone is flatter. Your energy is off. Your expression is slightly wrong. They can't explain it, but they feel it. And they respond to it.

The reset is not complicated. It takes thirty seconds. Take a breath. Check your posture. Clear the last interaction. Remind yourself that this person just pulled onto the lot and has no idea what happened ten minutes ago — and they don't deserve to pay for it. That small mental reset changes everything about how the next greeting lands.

The Wrong Opening Question

Covered in the previous chapter, but worth repeating here because it belongs on this list. "What are you looking to buy today?" asks the customer to commit before they're ready. "How can I help you today?" invites them to tell you where they are. One builds a wall. The other opens a door. Know the difference and make sure you're always opening the door.

Disappearing After the Greeting

This one is less about the first sixty seconds and more about the sixty seconds after them. You greet the customer. They say they're just looking. You say, "Sure, take your time." And then you vanish.

You don't make eye contact again. You don't check in. You drift back to your desk, your phone, or a conversation with a colleague. And the customer, who was just starting to relax, now isn't sure where the person who greeted them went or whether they can get help if they want it.

Stay available. Not hovering — that's a different mistake. But present. Visible. Easy to approach. The customer who says they're just looking often becomes the customer who asks a question three minutes later — if someone nearby looks ready to help.

FROM THE FLOOR

I walked into a well-known furniture store one afternoon looking for a recliner. Had a specific one in mind. Knew what I wanted to spend. Ready to buy.

Three salespeople were sitting on a showroom couch. I could hear them — in earshot, not trying to be quiet — debating whose turn it was to help me. Like I was an interruption to whatever they were doing.

The one who drew the short straw walked over. No greeting. No name. No smile. Just: "What are you here to buy today?"

I said: Nothing. I'm just looking. I'll let you know if I need help."

And I meant it. They'd lost me in the first five seconds. I didn't buy a thing there. Went somewhere else and bought the same recliner the same afternoon.

The irony is, I walked in ready to spend money. All they had to do was make me feel like a person, not a chore. Instead, they spent more energy arguing over whose turn it was than they spent on the customer standing in front of them. That's not a sales problem. That's a culture problem. And it starts—and ends—with how a team treats the greeting.

"The Rule: The mistakes that kill the first minute are almost always invisible to the person making them. Name them, know them, and catch them in yourself before the customer catches them for you."

CHAPTER 9

WHEN CUSTOMERS SAY I'M JUST LOOKING

EVERY CAR SALESPERSON HEARS it. You walk up, you introduce yourself, you ask how you can help — and the customer looks at you and says: "I'm just looking."

New salespeople almost always hear that as rejection. It isn't. In thirty-five years in this business, I've heard that phrase more times than I can count. And the one thing I can tell you with confidence is that it rarely means what salespeople think it means.

What the Phrase Actually Means

"I'm just looking" is a protective response. It's the verbal equivalent of putting your hands up. The customer is saying, in the most polite way they know: I'm not ready to be sold to yet. I need a minute. Don't rush me.

It is seldom a statement of final disinterest. Think about it — customers who have zero interest in buying a car don't usually pull onto a dealership lot and get out of their vehicle. The fact that they're standing on your lot means something. They came for a reason. "I'm just looking" is not that reason. It's the shield they raise while they figure out whether this is a safe environment to share the reason.

Your job when you hear it is not to overcome it, push through it, or pretend it wasn't said. Your job is to honor it and stay available. Because the customer who feels like their request for space was respected is far more likely to come back to you when they're ready than the customer who feels like that request was ignored.

The Right Response

The correct response to "I'm just looking" is simple and pressure-free:

"That's perfectly fine. Take all the time you need. I'll be nearby if you see something you want to take a closer look at."

That's it. No pivot. No follow-up question was designed to keep them talking. No "Well, while you're looking, let me just show you this one thing." Just a clean, genuine acknowledgment that respects what they said and leaves the door open.

Then give them actual space. Don't hover at four feet. Don't track their movement around the lot like you're watching inventory. Let them move through the space on their own terms. Stay visible and available, but not present in a way that creates pressure.

What happens next, more often than most salespeople expect, is that the customer comes back. They have a question. They found something they want to look at more closely. They've decided on their own that you seem approachable and would like some help. The wall came down not because you pushed it — but because you didn't. That distinction matters more than most people in this business appreciate.

A Gentle Follow-Up That Works

There are times when a low-pressure follow-up can gently keep the conversation alive without feeling pushy. The keyword is gentle. This only works if the customer seems receptive—not if they've clearly signaled they want to be left alone.

Something like: "Are you comparing a few different models today, or did something specific bring you in?"

That question is conversational rather than transactional. It invites the customer to share where they are in the process without requiring a commitment. Some will open up. Others will repeat that they're just looking—which is fine. You acknowledge it again and give them space again. The point is that you tried in a low-pressure way, and the customer felt respected either way.

Sometimes It Really Is About You

I want to be straight about something that most sales training glosses over. Sometimes "I'm just looking" is a response to something specific about the interaction — the pace of your approach, the tone of your greeting, a question that felt too aggressive. Sometimes the customer is reacting to you, not just to the environment.

That's information worth having. If you're consistently hearing "I'm just looking" as your first response, it's worth asking yourself what in your approach might be triggering it. Too fast? Too loud? Wrong opening question? Is your energy coming off as desperate rather than confident?

And sometimes it genuinely isn't about anything you did. Sometimes a customer connects with one salesperson and not another for reasons that have nothing to do with skill or approach.

FROM THE FLOOR

I had a colleague who couldn't get any traction with a woman at the used-car lot. She kept saying she was just looking. He couldn't figure out what was off — he'd done everything right as far as he could tell. He came and got me.

I went out, introduced myself, and asked how I could help her.

She said, "Thank God you're here. I really want to buy this car. But that other guy looks exactly like my ex-husband, and I cannot stand the sight of him."

Nothing to do with the car. Nothing to do with the approach. She knew exactly what she wanted — she just needed a different person in front of her before she was going to let the conversation happen. We tested the vehicle, worked out fair numbers, and she drove home happy.

Don't take "I'm just looking" personally. Don't take it as a verdict. Take it as information — something needs to be adjusted. Sometimes that's your approach. Sometimes it's giving more space. And occasionally it's a different person entirely. All of those are workable. None of them is the end of the deal.

"The Rule: 'I'm just looking" is not rejection. It is a request for space. Honor it, stay available, and let the customer come to you when they're ready. Most of them will."

CHAPTER 10

THE FIRST SIXTY SECONDS AND CUSTOMER CONFIDENCE

THERE IS A VERSION of the car sales process that feels easy. The conversation flows naturally, the customer is engaged and forthcoming, and by the time you're sitting down with numbers, the foundation feels solid. And there is a version where everything is harder than it should be — where the customer is guarded, answers are short, and the whole interaction feels like you're pushing against resistance that never quite goes away.

The difference between those two experiences is almost always the first sixty seconds.

When the opening is right — when the customer feels comfortable, respected, and confident in the person they're working with from the start — the rest of the process benefits from that momentum. When the opening is wrong, you spend the rest of the interaction trying to recover ground that was lost before the conversation really began.

What Customer Confidence Actually Looks Like

Customer confidence in the first 60 seconds doesn't mean the customer is ready to buy. It means the customer feels safe enough to keep talking. Safe enough to share what they're actually looking for. Safe enough to ask the questions they came in with. Safe enough to stay engaged rather than retreating behind short answers and deflections.

That safety gets communicated through small signals in the opening moments. Your composure tells them there's no reason to be tense. Your pace tells them you're not going to rush them. Your eye contact tells them you're genuinely present. Your opening question tells them you're there to help, not to extract. When those signals appear together in the first 60 seconds, something shifts in the customer. The guard comes down. The conversation becomes more real.

Composure Is Contagious

Here is something I observed early in my career and never forgot: a calm salesperson creates calm customers. An anxious salesperson creates anxious customers.

This is not a metaphor. It's how human interaction actually works. People regulate their emotional state partly by the signals they receive from those around them. When you approach a customer with genuine calm — not performed calm, not forced calm, but the real composure of someone comfortable in their environment and confident in what they're doing — customers tend to match that energy. Their shoulders drop a little. Their answers get a little longer. They start to look around the lot with curiosity rather than caution.

When you approach with anxiety or desperation, the opposite happens. The customer's guard goes up to match the customer's. They become more careful about what they say. They give shorter answers. They start looking for an exit.

You cannot always control how a customer arrives. You can control what they encounter when they get there. Your composure in the first sixty seconds is one of the most powerful tools you have — and it costs you nothing to use it.

Clarity Builds Confidence

Customers want to feel that the person helping them knows what they're doing. Not just knows the inventory — knows the process. Knows what comes next. Knows how to handle what the customer is about to ask.

That confidence in your process communicates itself through how you move through the opening. When your greeting is clear and unhurried, your introduction is direct and easy to hear, and your first question is focused and purposeful, customers feel they're in the hands of someone who has done this before and done it well. That feeling matters. It lowers the customer's uncertainty about the process itself, which is one of the biggest sources of resistance in the early stages of a car purchase.

Conversely, when the greeting is fumbled, when the salesperson seems unsure of what to say or how to proceed, customers pick up on that uncertainty immediately. It raises their own. It makes them less likely to trust the process and more likely to stay guarded.

The first sixty seconds are your opportunity to establish that you are a professional who knows what you're doing and is there to make this easier for them. Take it seriously. Prepare for it. Execute it cleanly.

The Momentum Effect

Here's the practical payoff of getting the first sixty seconds right: momentum. A conversation that starts well tends to keep going well. A customer who feels comfortable and confident in the opening is more likely to stay engaged, ask more questions, share more about their situation, and remain open to your guidance as the process moves forward.

That momentum is easier to maintain than it is to create from scratch after a weak opening. Every positive signal in the first minute — every small thing you do that makes the customer feel comfortable rather than guarded — adds to the foundation on which the rest of the interaction is built.

Master the first sixty seconds consistently, and you'll notice something has changed in your numbers. Not because you suddenly know more about the vehicles or became a better closer overnight. But because more of your conversations start from a place of comfort and trust, and conversations that start that way close at a higher rate than the ones that don't.

FROM THE FLOOR

One afternoon, a customer pulled into the lot in a taxi. That caught my attention — most people drive themselves in. This one stepped out and walked directly toward a specific vehicle, as if he already knew exactly what he was looking for.

I didn't rush. I stood up, walked out at a normal pace, and gave him a small wave as I crossed the lot. When I reached him, I introduced myself and told him I'd be glad to help if he had any questions.

He told me he'd just gotten off a flight and came straight from the airport. His vehicle was destroyed in a parking lot fire while he was traveling. He'd seen one of our ads and came directly to us. He knew which vehicle he wanted. He just needed to drive it and confirm it.

We took a short test drive. Came back. He asked how to make out the check.

Start to finish, maybe forty-five minutes. The deal was easy because the approach was right. No pressure, no assumptions, no rushing. Just a professional greeting and a willingness to follow the customer's lead.

Not every customer comes in ready to buy. But every customer deserves that same professional opening. You never know which one is going to be the taxi customer — the one who's already decided and just needs someone not to get in their way.

"The Rule: A strong first sixty seconds creates momentum that carries through the entire sale. Get the opening right, and the rest of the process becomes easier. Let it go wrong, and you're working uphill for the next hour."

CHAPTER 11

A Simple Meet and Greet Script for Car Sales

EVERY SALESPERSON, AT SOME point, wants to know the exact words to use. Just give me the line. Tell me what to say. Give me the script.

I understand the impulse. When you're new to the lot or working through a situation you haven't encountered before, having a reliable structure to fall back on is genuinely useful. The problem isn't wanting a script. The problem is treating it like a performance to deliver rather than a framework to internalize.

The salespeople who sound scripted sound that way because they're reciting something. The salespeople who have truly internalized a structure — who understand what each element is trying to accomplish and have put it into their own voice through practice and repetition — don't sound scripted at all. They sound like professionals who know exactly what they're doing. That's the goal.

The Five-Element Structure

Every strong car sales meet-and-greet follows five elements in sequence. None of them is optional. All of them are trainable.

First: the acknowledgment. Before you reach the customer, let them know you've seen them. A nod, a small wave, a brief verbal signal from a distance. This happens the moment they arrive, before you move.

Second: the approach. Move toward them at a calm, purposeful pace. Hands relaxed and visible, head up, phone away. Stop at a conversational distance — close enough to talk normally, far enough that they don't feel crowded.

Third: the introduction. Your name and the dealership name, said clearly. Not rushed, not mumbled. Your name is what makes this interaction personal. It creates accountability and connection. Say it as it matters — because it does.

Fourth: the service question. Open, non-threatening, focused on helping rather than selling. "How can I help you today?" is the standard. It works because it invites the customer to speak in their own terms without pressure.

Fifth: the listen. Ask the question and stop talking. Let the customer answer completely, at their own pace, without interruption. This is the hardest part for most salespeople and the most important.

What It Sounds Like on the Lot

In practice, the script sounds something like this for a single customer:

"Hi, welcome in. My name is [your name] with [dealership name] — how can I help you today?"

For a couple or group:

"Hello, welcome in — good to see you both. My name is [your name]. How can I help you today?"

And immediately after, if you haven't confirmed it yet:

"Have you been in before, or is this your first time visiting us?"

Simple. Clean. Nothing wasted. Everything that needs to happen in the opening thirty seconds is covered in those lines.

Adapting to Context

The structure stays the same. The delivery adapts to what's in front of you.

On a hot afternoon: "Welcome in — come on out of this heat. My name is [your name] — how can I help you?" On a rainy day, when the customer walks in wet, "Welcome in — glad you made it through that. I'm [your name] — how can I help you today?" When a couple comes in, and one of them hasn't introduced themselves: "And you are?" Two words. Acknowledges the person. Costs nothing.

The framework is a map, not a script. It ensures you cover what needs to be covered — the acknowledgment, the introduction, the service question, the listen — while leaving room for you to be a person rather than a recording.

How to Make It Yours

Read the structure. Understand what each element is trying to accomplish. Then rewrite every line in your own words — the words that feel natural to you, that fit how you actually talk, that don't sound like you're reading from a card.

Then practice it out loud. Not in your head — out loud. Record yourself and listen back. Does it sound natural? Does it sound like you? Ask a colleague to play the customer and run through it until it stops feeling like a performance and starts feeling like the way you start conversations.

This takes time: weeks, not days. But once the structure is internalized — once you're no longer thinking about the steps and are just having a conversation — your meet-and-greet becomes noticeably more confident, more consistent, and more effective. Not because you said different words. Because you said the right words in a way that sounded like you.

Consistency Is the Skill

The script doesn't earn its value with the easy customer who walks in ready to talk. It earns it with the guarded customer, the distracted customer, and the customer who walked in expecting the worst. With those customers, structure keeps you on track when improvisation would let you down.

The salesperson who follows the framework 90% of the time gets 90% results at best. The ones who do it right with every customer — not because it feels necessary every time, but because it's the standard they hold themselves to — those are the ones whose numbers reflect it over time.

Consistency is the skill. The script is how you build it.

"The Rule: Don't recite the script. Own it. Put it in your voice, practice until it's automatic, and run it every time with every customer — especially the ones who make it feel optional."

Chapter 12

The Psychology Behind the First Minute

EVERYTHING IN THIS BOOK comes back to one thing: the person on the other side of the interaction. The techniques, the structure, the script, the body language — all of it is a framework for guiding a human being through a moment that most of them find uncomfortable. The framework works because people work a certain way. The more clearly you understand how people work, the more effective every tool in this book becomes.

The Customer Arrived Nervous

Before a customer steps out of their car, they've already been having a conversation in their head about what this experience is going to be like. For most of them, that conversation includes some version of the following: this might be uncomfortable, someone is probably going to pressure me, I don't want to make a decision I'll regret, and I'd rather be in control of this than feel like I'm being managed through it.

They've heard the stories. Their friends warned them. Some of them have been burned before and are giving the industry a cautious second chance. They arrive with their guard partially up. Not fully — they came, after all. But enough that the first sixty seconds have real work to do.

The entire opening sequence we've built in this book — the acknowledgment from a distance, the purposeful approach, the introduction, the service question, the patient listen — is designed to do one thing: lower that guard before the conversation asks anything of the customer. When you succeed at that, everything that follows becomes easier. When you don't, you're fighting resistance for the rest of the interaction.

The Gap Between What You Know and What They Know

Here is something worth understanding deeply, because it explains much of the friction in the early stages of a car purchase.

You do this every day. The process — the steps, the language, the sequence of events from greeting to delivery — is completely familiar to you. You've done it hundreds or thousands of times. It feels routine.

To the customer, none of it is routine. They buy a car every three to ten years. The terminology is foreign. The process is opaque. They don't know what comes after the test drive, or why the desk manager gets involved, or what the finance office is going to try to sell them. They're navigating a process that you find completely ordinary, and for them it's genuinely unfamiliar.

That gap — between your familiarity and their unfamiliarity — is a major source of the caution they arrive with. People are uncomfortable in situations they don't understand. Your job in the first sixty seconds is to start closing that gap. Not by explaining every step of the process in detail — that would be overwhelming. But by being clear enough, calm enough, and professional enough that the customer begins to feel: I don't know exactly how this works, but I think this person does, and I think they're going to be straight with me about it.

That feeling is trust. And it starts forming in the first minute, based almost entirely on how you handle the opening.

People Want to Be Led, Not Pressured

This is the most counterintuitive principle in this entire book, so it's worth sitting with it for a minute.

Customers don't want to be pressured. But most of them — more than you'd expect — do want to be led. There is a significant difference between the two, and it matters enormously in car sales.

Pressure means trying to force someone toward a decision they're not ready to make in a way that overrides their judgment. That creates resistance and damages trust. Leading means guiding someone through a process they don't fully understand, in a way that respects their judgment while providing the direction they need. That feels like service. And customers will follow a confident, trustworthy professional through an unfamiliar process — because that's exactly what they came for.

Your customer buys a car every few years. You do this every day. You are the expert in this situation. When you act like one — when you're calm, organized, clear about what comes next, and genuinely interested in helping this specific person find the right vehicle — customers feel safe following you. That is not manipulation. That is professional service done well.

The moment you start deferring to the customer on process questions they don't know the answers to, or acting uncertain about what should happen next, the whole thing gets wobbly. Stay grounded. Know the process. Lead the way. That's what they need from you, even if they couldn't articulate it.

They Remember How You Made Them Feel

Customers don't remember every detail of a car-buying experience. They may forget your exact words in the greeting. They may forget the specific question you asked. But they remember how the experience made them feel — and that emotional impression, formed largely in the first few minutes, shapes whether they come back, whether they refer others, and what they say about the dealership when someone they know is looking for a car.

Two dealerships can sell the same vehicle at the same price. The one that makes people feel respected, comfortable, and genuinely helped is almost always the one that earns the long-term business. The first sixty seconds are where that feeling starts. Get them right, and you're building something that lasts beyond the transaction. Get them wrong, and you're starting a deficit that most customers never fully forgive.

"The Rule: Customers don't remember exactly what you said in the first minute. They remember how it felt. Make it feel like the beginning of something good."

Chapter 13

The First Minute Checklist

CHECKLISTS EXIST BECAUSE CONSISTENCY is hard. Not because salespeople are careless — but because maintaining a high standard across every customer interaction, across an entire shift, across weeks and months of doing the same job, is genuinely difficult. Habits drift. Energy fluctuates. The tenth customer of the day doesn't automatically get the same quality opening as the first unless there's a standard in place that ensures that consistency.

A mental checklist is the standard. It takes less than ten seconds to run through before every customer interaction. It prevents most of the mistakes covered in this book. And it turns good intentions into repeatable behavior — which is the only kind of behavior that shows up in your numbers over time.

Run through this before every customer arrives. Not some of the time. Every time.

✓ Appearance is professional and appropriate for the environment. — You look like someone worth doing business with before you've said a word.

✓ Phone is put away. — Not in your hand, not visible. Away. Before you approach, not as you approach.

✓ You acknowledged the customer before approaching. — A nod, a wave, a brief verbal signal. They know they've been seen before you've taken a step.

✓ You gave them a moment to settle. — They stepped out of the car and had a few seconds to orient themselves before you moved.

✓ You approached at a normal, purposeful pace. — Not running. Not dragging. The pace of someone glad they showed up.

✓ You introduced yourself clearly by name. — Said once, distinctly. Your name makes the interaction personal and creates accountability.

✓ You asked how you can help — not what they're here to buy. — Open, service-oriented, non-threatening. Their answer tells you where to start.

✓ You acknowledged everyone in the group. — Every person who walks in gets a greeting. No one stands there feeling invisible.

✓ You asked whether they've been in before. — Before you go any further. This protects your colleagues and the customer relationship.

✓ You stopped talking and listened to the answer. — Fully. Without interrupting. Without preparing your next line while they're still talking.

Ten Items. Every Customer. Every Time.

None of them is complicated. All of them are trainable. The salespeople who run this list consistently — not most of the time, every time — outperform the ones who do eight out of ten and think that's close enough.

Close enough is not the standard. Every time is the standard.

Using This Checklist in Your Daily Routine

The most effective way to use this checklist is to run it mentally in the few seconds between noticing a customer arriving and beginning to move toward them. That window — the moment when you see a car pull in and before you've taken a step — is exactly the right time for a fast internal check. Phone away? Posture right? Ready to acknowledge? Good. Now move.

Over time, running the checklist becomes automatic. You stop thinking about the individual items and start simply arriving at each customer interaction prepared. That's the goal—not the checklist itself, but the standard it trains you to hold. When the checklist disappears into habit, what's left is a professional who consistently makes strong first impressions without having to work at it anymore.

That level of consistency is what separates the salespeople who always seem to have momentum from the ones whose results depend on which side of the bed they got out of that morning. The checklist is how you build it. The habit is what pays for it.

"The Rule: Ten items. Every customer. Every time. The checklist is not the goal — the habit is. Run it until you don't have to think about it anymore."

CONCLUSTION

We've covered a lot of ground in this book. The moment before the customer leaves their car. The silent questions they're asking as they pull onto the lot. The ten-second window in which first impressions form. The approach that communicates confidence without pressure. The opening sequence that builds comfort before the conversation asks the customer for anything. The body language that answers trust questions before you've said a word. The first question opens rather than closes. The mistakes that kill the first minute without the salesperson ever realizing it. What "I'm just looking" actually means. The script you make your own. The psychology underneath all of it. The checklist that turns good intentions into consistent behavior.

All of it connects back to one thing: the first sixty seconds determine what kind of conversation the next sixty minutes will be.

What Changes When You Get This Right

When the first sixty seconds are handled well — consistently, professionally, with genuine attention to the customer in front of you — something measurable happens to your results. Not because you suddenly know more about the inventory. Not because you developed a better close overnight. But because more of your conversations start from a foundation of comfort and trust, conversations that start that way close at a higher rate than conversations that don't.

Customers who feel comfortable in the first minute ask more questions. They share more about their situation. They stay engaged longer. They're more willing to be guided through the process. And when the numbers conversation happens, they're working with you rather than against you — because the relationship was established before the transaction was ever discussed.

That's the practical value of mastering the first minute. It doesn't just make the opening feel better. It makes everything after it easier.

What This Requires

Mastering the first minute requires preparation, not talent. It requires deciding, before every shift, that you're going to show up ready. That your posture will be right when the first customer arrives. That your phone is going to be away. That you're going to acknowledge the next person who pulls in, approach at the right pace, introduce yourself clearly, ask the right question, and actually listen to the answer.

None of that is complicated. All of it is a choice. And the choice has to be made consistently — not on the days when you're feeling sharp, and the lot is busy, and everything is going well. Still, on the slow Tuesday afternoons when the energy is low and it's tempting to let your standards slip because nobody seems to be watching.

The customers are always watching. Every single person who pulls onto that lot is evaluating the environment from the moment they arrive. What they see in those first sixty seconds shapes what they decide about you, about the dealership, and about whether this is going to be the experience they were hoping for or the one they were warned about.

Give them the right answer every time. Not because it's easy. Because it's the standard.

The Simplest Summary

Acknowledge them before you approach. Give them a moment to settle. Walk toward them with purpose and calm. Say your name clearly. Ask how you can help. Listen to what they say. Greet everyone who walks in with them. Stay available without hovering.

That's the first minute. Simple enough to describe in two sentences. Powerful enough to change your results when you do it right with every customer, every day, without exception.

The sale begins the moment they see you. Make sure what they see is worth staying for.

— *Bruce Huddleston*

Tips For The Manager

Building a Team That Gets the First Minute Right

The first sixty seconds of a customer interaction are too important to leave to chance — or to each salesperson's individual interpretation of what a good greeting looks like. As a sales manager, you have more influence over what happens in that first minute than anyone else on the floor. The question is whether you're using it.

Observe Before You Coach

The most effective managers spend time watching how their salespeople approach customers — not from inside the showroom, but from a position where they can see the actual interaction unfold. What does the approach look like from the customer's perspective? How fast is the salesperson moving? Where is their phone? Are they acknowledging the whole group or just the person who spoke first? What does their expression look like when they arrive?

Most salespeople have no idea what their own greeting looks like from ten feet away. A manager who can describe it specifically — not "you need to be more confident" but "you're arriving before the customer has closed the car door, and they're already backed up against the vehicle by the time you introduce yourself" — gives the salesperson something concrete to change. Specific feedback changes behavior. Vague feedback doesn't.

Make Role Play a Regular Practice

Role-play is one of the most effective tools for improving greeting behavior and one of the most underused in automotive sales. Salespeople resist

it because it feels awkward. That awkwardness is exactly why it works —
it surfaces the habits and hesitations that don't show up in conversation
but do show up in front of customers.

Run greeting scenarios regularly. A single customer. A couple where
one person hasn't been introduced. A customer who says they're just
looking. A customer who gets out of the car and immediately starts
walking toward a specific vehicle. A salesperson who just had a difficult
interaction and needs to reset before the next customer arrives. The
more situations salespeople practice, the more flexible and confident
their actual greetings become.

Set the Standard Visibly

Teams become what their leadership notices and rewards. If strong
greetings are observed, acknowledged, and discussed — if a manager
pulls a salesperson aside and says "I watched how you handled that family
that came in this afternoon, that was exactly right" — the behavior
becomes part of the culture. If greeting quality is never mentioned, it
becomes one of those things everyone knows they should do, but nobody
holds themselves accountable for.

Set the standard explicitly. Tell your team what a strong first minute
looks like. Use the checklist in Chapter Thirteen as a coaching framework. Track which items are consistently being hit and which keep
getting skipped. Make the meet-and-greet a regular topic in your training
conversations, not a one-time orientation item that nobody revisits.

Model It Yourself

The most powerful thing a sales manager can do to improve greeting
quality on their team is to demonstrate what a great opening looks like
in real interactions. When the manager greets a customer with the same
calm professionalism they expect from their salespeople, the whole team
watches. When they don't — when they're distracted, or rushed, or
handle an opening in a way that contradicts what they've been coaching
— the team watches that too.

Leadership communicates through behavior more than through instruction. If you want a team that takes the first minute seriously, take it seriously yourself every time you interact with a customer on the floor or the lot.

Bulk Training With This Series

The Car Sales Survival Guide Series is designed to work as a complete onboarding and development system for sales teams. Each book goes deep on one specific skill — the meet-and-greet, the first 60 seconds, handling objections, body language, closing, follow-up — in a format that can be read quickly and referenced regularly.

Dealerships that use the series as structured training material find that new salespeople develop foundational skills more quickly and that experienced salespeople identify specific areas to sharpen. Bulk pricing is available for dealerships and sales organizations.

www.bedrockheritagepublishing.com

info@bedrockheritagepublishing.com

www.carsalessurvivalseries.com

Appendix—The Rules

Every chapter of this book ended with a rule. Here they are collected in one place — a quick-reference summary of the principles that matter most.

Introduction — *"The Rule: The sale doesn't begin when you start talking. It begins the moment the customer sees you. Everything after that is either easier or harder, depending on what happened in those first sixty seconds."*

Chapter One — *"The Rule: The sale begins the moment the customer pulls onto the lot. Be ready before they arrive, because by the time they step out of that car, they've already started deciding how this is going to go."*

Chapter Two — *"The Rule: Every customer arrives with a question they haven't asked yet. Your job in the first sixty seconds is to answer it before they do: yes, this is someone I can trust."*

Chapter Three — *"The Rule: Ten seconds. That's how fast the first impression forms on the lot. Be the salesperson they decide they want to talk to before you've opened your mouth."*

Chapter Four — *"The Rule: Attentive and aggressive are not the same thing. Give the customer a moment, walk with purpose, and arrive as someone they're glad showed up."*

Chapter Five — *"The Rule: The perfect opening is not a performance. It is a sequence done consistently — acknowledge, approach, introduce, ask, and listen. Do it right every time, and the conversation takes care of itself."*

Chapter Six — *"The Rule: Your body language answers the customer's questions before you open your mouth. Make sure the answers it's giving are the ones that open the conversation."*

Chapter Seven — *"The Rule: The first question either opens the conversation or closes it. Ask how you can help, stop talking, and let the customer tell you everything you need to know."*

Chapter Eight — *"The Rule: The mistakes that kill the first minute are almost always invisible to the person making them. Name them, know them, and catch them in yourself before the customer catches them for you."*

Chapter Nine — *"The Rule: 'I'm just looking" is not rejection. It is a request for space. Honor it, stay available, and let the customer come to you when they're ready. Most of them will."*

Chapter Ten — *"The Rule: A strong first sixty seconds creates momentum that carries through the entire sale. Get the opening right, and the rest of the process becomes easier. Let it go wrong, and you're working uphill for the next hour."*

Chapter Eleven — *"The Rule: Don't recite the script. Own it. Put it in your voice, practice until it's automatic, and run it every time with every customer — especially the ones who make it feel optional."*

Chapter Twelve — *"The Rule: Customers don't remember exactly what you said in the first minute. They remember how it felt. Make it feel like the beginning of something good."*

Chapter Thirteen — *"The Rule: Ten items. Every customer. Every time. The checklist is not the goal — the habit is. Run it until you don't have to think about it anymore."*

ALSO AVAILABLE

By Bruce Huddleston

The First 60 Seconds in Car Sales is part of the Car Sales Survival Guide Series — a collection of focused training guides, each going deep on one specific sales skill. Each book is designed to stand alone as a focused training resource or to be used as part of a complete system for onboarding and developing sales staff.

The Complete Car Sales Survival Guide

The No-BS Playbook for New Automotive Salespeople

CAR SALES SURVIVAL GUIDE SERIES

The Meet and Greet Playbook

How to Make Powerful First Impressions with Customers, Clients, and Guests

The First 60 Seconds in Car Sales

A Proven Meet and Greet System to Build Trust and Start More Conversations

How to Handle "I'm Just Looking" in Car Sales

A Simple System to Turn Brush-Offs into Productive Conversations

Body Language in Car Sales

How Posture, Eye Contact, and Presence Build Customer Trust

Greeting Customers on the Lot

How to Approach Buyers Without Pressure

The Ten-Second Rule in Car Sales

Why First Impressions Determine Whether Customers Stay or Leave

The Car Sales Conversation Starter Guide

How to Begin Natural Conversations That Lead to Sales

Car Sales Confidence for New Salespeople

How to Approach Customers Without Fear or Hesitation

Common Car Sales Greeting Mistakes

What Drives Customers Away in the First Minute

The First Five Minutes With a Car Buyer

How to Transition from Greeting to Conversation and Move Toward the Sale

Order individual copies or inquire about bulk pricing:

www.bedrockheritagepublishing.com

info@bedrockheritagepublishing.com

Work With Bruce

Coaching and Group Training

This book is a starting point. For salespeople and teams who want to go deeper — working through the material personally, applying it to their specific situation, and building the habits that make it stick — Bruce offers individual and group sessions through Life Guidance Consulting LLC.

One-on-One Coaching

Individual sessions for salespeople at any stage of their career. Whether you're in your first ninety days on the floor or you've been selling for years and want to break through a plateau, one-on-one coaching gives you direct access to thirty-five years of real-world experience — applied specifically to your situation, your dealership, and your goals.

Group Training Sessions

Group sessions for sales teams working through The First 60 Seconds in Car Sales or the Car Sales Survival Guide Series together. Ideal for dealership onboarding, team development, and ongoing skills training. Sessions are practical, direct, and built around real scenarios from the sales floor—not theory.

Bulk Book Orders

Dealerships and sales organizations interested in using The First 60 Seconds in Car Sales or the Car Sales Survival Guide Series as structured onboarding or training materials can inquire about bulk pricing and customized packages.

Life Guidance Consulting LLC

www.lifeguidanceconsulting.com
bruce@lifeguidanceconsulting.com
For book orders and publishing inquiries:
www.bedrockheritagepublishing.com
info@bedrockheritagepublishing.com

About the Author

Bruce Huddleston spent thirty-five years in the automotive industry, working every level of the business from showroom floor salesperson to finance manager, sales manager, used car manager, and general manager. His career included new-car franchise dealerships, independent used-car operations, and a decade in buy-here, pay-here — giving him a breadth of experience that few in the industry can match.

He began as a high school dropout who needed a job and ended up discovering a profession. He ended as a veteran who had trained hundreds of salespeople, managed multiple departments, and built a reputation for straight talk in an industry that doesn't always reward it.

Since retiring, Bruce has opened a life coaching practice, assists his wife with her mental health therapy practice, and operates Bedrock Heritage Publishing, a division of Life Guidance Consulting LLC, where he writes practical guides for sales professionals across multiple industries.

The Complete Car Sales Survival Guide is his flagship work. The Car Sales Survival Guide Series — a collection of focused training guides on specific sales skills — is built on the same foundation of real experience, honest insight, and zero tolerance for the kind of nonsense that gives sales a bad name.

He lives in Tyler, Texas.

www.lifeguidanceconsulting.com

www.bedrockheritagepublishing.com

www.carsalessurvivalseries.com

A Quick Favor

If The First 60 Seconds in Car Sales gave you something useful — a technique that clicked, a habit that changed how you open conversations, a framework that made your first minute noticeably stronger — the single best thing you can do to help other salespeople find it is leave an honest review on Amazon.

It takes about two minutes. It makes a real difference to how the book gets discovered. And it helps the next salesperson who needs this information actually find it.

You can simply scan the QR code below.

*https://www.amazon.com/rev
iew/create-review/?asin=197
2179101*

https://www.amazon.com/review/create-review/?asin=1972179101

Thank you for reading.

Bruce Huddleston